DATE DUE	BORROWER'S NAME
	Rodrigo Crespo

D1289024

Weather Watching

Text: Sharon Dalgleish

Consultant: Richard Whitaker, Senior Meteorologist,
Bureau of Meteorology, Sydney, Australia

This edition first published 2003 by

MASON CREST PUBLISHERS INC.

370 Reed Road
Broomall, PA 19008

© Weldon Owen Inc.
Conceived and produced by

Weldon Owen Pty Limited

Library of Congress Cataloging-in-Publication Data
on file at the Library of Congress
ISBN: 1-59084-197-2

Printed in Singapore.
1 2 3 4 5 6 7 8 9 06 05 04 03

CONTENTS

Chinese
Storm-gods

WEATHER MYTHS

Long before science was able to help us understand the weather, people told stories to try to explain its frightening events. Around the world, different powerful gods were thought to control the weather. When the Norse god, Thor, was angry he made thunder with his hammer. Some Native Americans believed giant Thunderbirds beat their wings to make thunder. A Chinese myth tells how the God of Thunder, the Master of the Rain, the Earl of the Wind, Mother Lightning, and the Little Boy of the Clouds work together to make a storm.

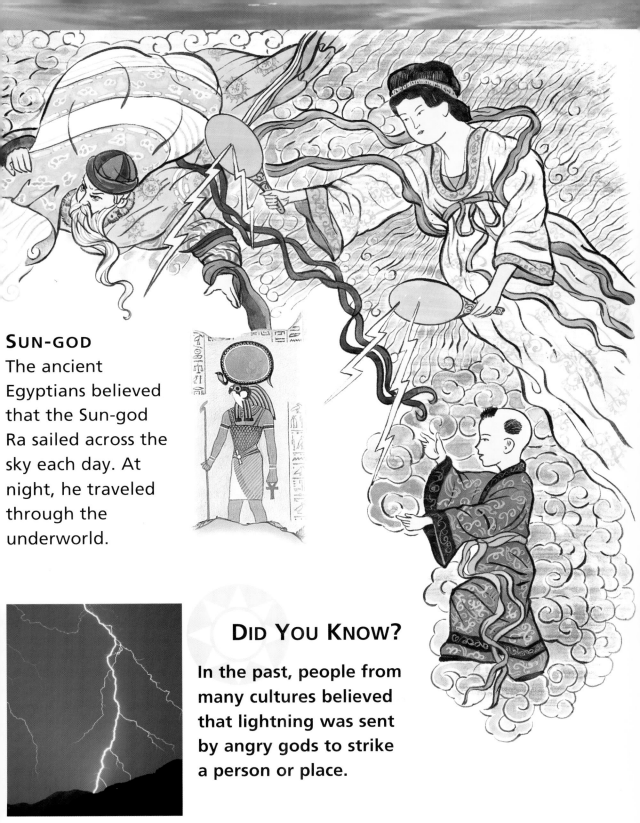

SUN-GOD

The ancient
Egyptians believed
that the Sun-god
Ra sailed across the
sky each day. At
night, he traveled
through the
underworld.

DID YOU KNOW?

In the past, people from
many cultures believed
that lightning was sent
by angry gods to strike
a person or place.

FORECASTING

Even though farmers and sailors have always observed the weather, they did not have instruments to measure it. This began to change in the 1600s when Galileo invented the thermometer. Then, in 1644, the barometer was invented to measure air pressure. Soon scientists had instruments to measure humidity and wind speed. Forecasting was becoming a science.

HOT AIR BALLOONS

The first manned balloon flights were made in 1783. Soon after, they were used to observe and study the weather. Brave balloonists risked their lives to fly the balloons and measure winds and temperatures in the upper atmosphere.

FORECASTING AS SCIENCE

These scientists from the 1600s
are measuring air pressure using
a barometer. The Academy of
Experiments in Florence, Italy, was
the center for studying the weather.

Today, weather conditions are measured and recorded every minute of the day and night. Observation stations, ships, planes, and satellites make sure that even remote areas are monitored. All this information is fed into a huge computer data bank. Meteorologists around the world use the data bank to prepare weather maps called synoptic charts. These charts show information about air pressure, wind speed and direction, cloud cover, temperature, and humidity. The charts take hours to prepare but they make possible the weather forecasts we see in the media.

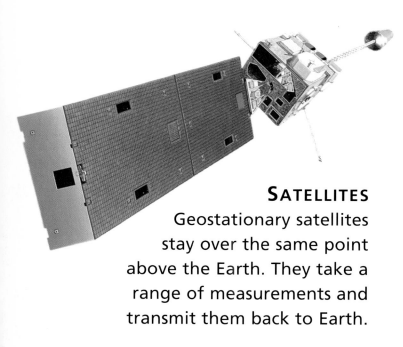

SATELLITES
Geostationary satellites stay over the same point above the Earth. They take a range of measurements and transmit them back to Earth.

A TYPICAL MEDIA WEATHER MAP

KEY TO SYMBOLS

wind symbols

⌐ light

⌐ high

⌐ gale force

weather symbols

snow | rain | cold front
fog | sleet | warm front
| | occluded front

cloud symbols

clear sky

partly cloudy

cloudy

Natural Clues

People have always looked to nature for signs about the weather. Many of these signs are based on superstition. Bees busily in flight are said to be a sign of fine weather. If the flowers of the morning glory are open, it means fine weather. If pine cones have their scales open, this also means it will stay fine and dry. Some grasshoppers tend to chirp during warm, dry weather. The louder they chirp, the hotter it will become. Sometimes information about the weather is in the form of rhymes passed from generation to generation.

"Red sky at night, a sailor's delight.
Red sky in the morning,
a sailor's warning."
Proverb

morning

night

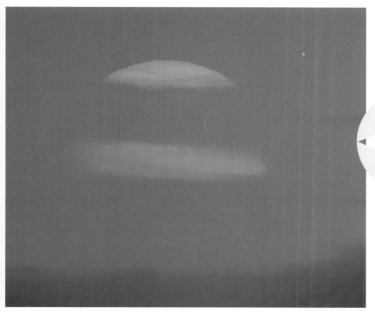

DID YOU KNOW?

Some people believe that a red sky at night means good weather and a red sky in the morning, bad weather. The red color is made when the clouds reflect the Sun when it is low in the sky.

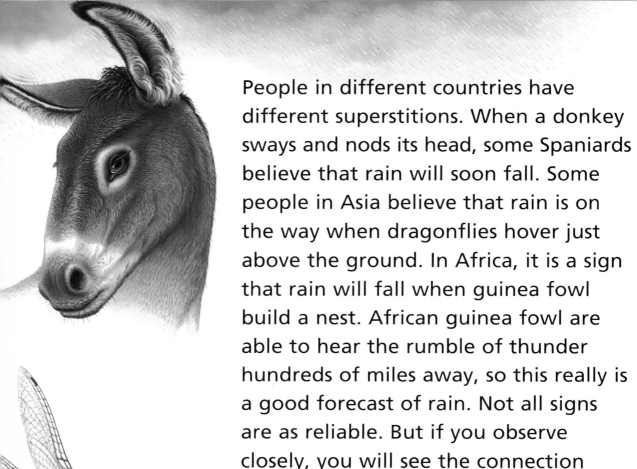

People in different countries have different superstitions. When a donkey sways and nods its head, some Spaniards believe that rain will soon fall. Some people in Asia believe that rain is on the way when dragonflies hover just above the ground. In Africa, it is a sign that rain will fall when guinea fowl build a nest. African guinea fowl are able to hear the rumble of thunder hundreds of miles away, so this really is a good forecast of rain. Not all signs are as reliable. But if you observe closely, you will see the connection between weather and nature.

SHOWER CATS

In Germany, some people believe that a cat washes itself just before a rain shower.

DID YOU KNOW?

Argiope spiders will not spin a web during heavy rain because it will damage their hard work. Some people believe that if this spider stops spinning, it means rain is coming.

MEASURING AND RECORDING

To find out what's really happening with the weather you need to measure different weather effects. Low air pressure often means rain or a storm. Air pressure is measured with a barometer. A simple barometer uses a water-filled glass tube. If water rises up the tube, low pressure is on the way. Humidity is the amount of water vapor in the air. It is measured with a hygrometer. Human hair expands in moist air so some hygrometers work by measuring the length of a hair!

RAINFALL

You can make a rain gauge by putting a funnel in a jar. Place it in the open to collect rainwater and measure rainfall. A pluviograph is more complicated. It plots the amount of rainfall on a chart.

WIND SPEED

Anemometers measure wind speed. The faster the cups spin, the higher the wind speed. In simple models, the number of rotations is counted by the observer. Other models can be connected to a computer for more accurate readings.

COMPUTER SUPPORT

Meteorologists use computers programmed to imitate weather conditions to predict weather patterns. You can use a computer to record and interpret your own weather observations.

WEATHER SCREEN

Thermometers should be kept in a shelter to shield them from direct sunlight. This makes the readings more accurate. If you become very good at keeping records, you may even become an official observer.

You can set up a simple weather station in a yard. Take instrument readings at the same time each day and record them in a weather diary. You might also want to include personal observations about wildlife and describe any unusual weather events, like lightning, hail, or fog. Recording all this information is the first step. Next you need to put it all together and make your forecast. Adding your own forecast to the forecast you hear on television will help you understand how the local weather will develop.

WEATHER ENGINE
The Sun's heat drives
all our weather.

SOLAR ENERGY

You would need 200 million power stations to generate an amount of energy similar to the amount of solar energy that reaches the Earth's atmosphere every 24 hours. Some of the energy coming from the Sun is absorbed by the Earth's surface. The rest makes its way back into the atmosphere by reflection and radiation. Different parts of the Earth reflect different amounts of heat. White snow reflects most of the energy, so very little heat is left. A dark green rain forest, however, absorbs a lot of energy. These differences help make pressure patterns that cause winds to blow and the atmosphere to circulate.

DID YOU KNOW?

The Earth is shaped like a ball, so the Sun's rays are stronger near the equator than at the poles. This is why the equator is hot and the polar regions are so cold.

AIR CURRENTS

The Sun heats the Earth, which in turn sends warm air back into the atmosphere. Cold air then drops to replace the rising warm air. This constant cycle of cold and warm air currents brings wind and rain.

Polar
The polar regions are the coldest parts of the world. Even though snow falls often, these areas are dry.

Subtropical
In summer these areas are hot and wet. In winter they are dry and mild.

Mountain
Mountain areas are often cold, wet, and windy. As you climb higher the atmosphere gets thinner and colder.

Wet Temperate
These areas have four seasons, with cool, wet winters and warm, wet summers.

Desert
Plants find it hard to survive in these areas because it is so hot and dry. At night it can be very cold.

WORLD CLIMATE

The climate of an area depends on its location on the round Earth. Close to the equator it is nearly always hot. Close to the poles it is always cold. The areas in between are called temperate zones. Those areas have warm summers and cool winters. Mountains are colder because they are higher. Sea breezes in coastal areas usually keep it from getting too cold or too hot.

Dry Temperate
It doesn't rain very often in these areas. They have mild winters and hot, dry summers.

Tropical
Low areas close to the equator are called tropical. They are hot and wet. In some areas it rains all year round.

Cold Temperate
These areas have long, cold winters with a lot of snow. Summers are often mild and damp.

POLES APART

The Arctic is a frozen sea around the North Pole. The Antarctic is a frozen continent around the South Pole.

purple areas show mountain zones

blue areas show polar zones

POLAR AND MOUNTAIN ZONES

Polar zones are covered in snow and ice all year round. In mountain zones, the weather can change quickly from bright and sunny to stormy. Each mountain has its own weather pattern. One side of a mountain can even have different weather from the other side of the same mountain. Mountains have an effect on the weather in other areas as well. They can block moving air masses and cause changes in temperature, humidity, and rainfall.

THE DEEP FREEZE

In polar zones, the white snow and ice reflect most of the heat from the Sun back into the atmosphere.

STRANGE BUT TRUE

The Arctic fox can change its color to suit the season. In winter its fur changes from smoky gray to white to camouflage the fox against the snow.

NORTH AND SOUTH

The temperate zones lie in two bands—one north and and one south of the equator.

green areas show temperate zones

TEMPERATE ZONES

Temperate zones have a climate that varies a lot because of the cool air blowing from the poles toward the tropical zones. There are four different seasons. Plants and animals have to adapt to these changes in the weather and food supply. In spring, plants begin to grow leaves and flowers. Animals start to breed. This growth continues until summer. As autumn gets closer, some trees drop their leaves. Many animals migrate or get ready to hibernate. In winter, there is less activity.

WARM TEMPERATE

The temperate zones closest to the equator are warmer.

COOL TEMPERATE

The temperate zones get cooler closer to the poles.

AMAZING!

The painted turtle makes its own antifreeze. The antifreeze stops ice from forming inside its organs in winter.

DESERT AND TROPICAL ZONES

Most deserts are hot in the day because the land is heated by the Sun. Clouds are rare, so at night the heat escapes back into the atmosphere. Then the temperature can drop to almost freezing. Some deserts also have freezing conditions in the day, because of cold winds. Even though not all deserts are hot, they are all dry.

Tropical zones are very different. They are usually hot and have high rainfall. Plants grow quickly. The lushest areas on Earth are in tropical zones.

AMAZING!

Poison-dart frogs live in tropical areas. These frogs carry their tadpoles on their back to a safe home high in the treetops.

AROUND THE WORLD

Tropical areas lie in a band centered on the equator. Deserts can be found on the borders of tropical areas, on the dry sides of mountain ranges, and in the centers of continents.

yellow areas show
desert zones

green areas show
tropical zones

A Changing World

The Earth's atmosphere works like a greenhouse. Gases in the atmosphere trap some of the heat from the Sun to warm the Earth. This greenhouse effect is important. Without it the Earth would be too cold for life. The Earth, however, is getting warmer. Some scientists believe this is because more carbon dioxide and other greenhouse gases are being released by human activity. As more gases fill the atmosphere, more heat is absorbed and the Earth becomes warmer and warmer.

GREENHOUSE GAS
Fuels that are burned to power cars and factories release carbon dioxide into the atmosphere. Even cows affect the atmosphere. They produce methane gas when they digest grass.

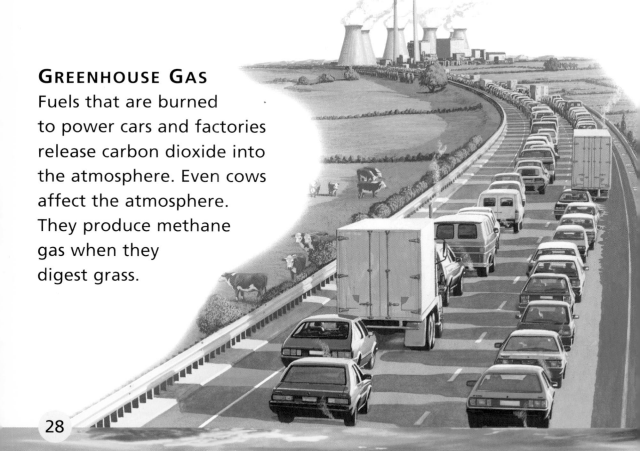

ICE AGES

The Earth's climate has changed many times. In the last million years there have been four main ice ages. Great slabs of ice pushed across the land.

EL NIÑO AND LA NIÑA

El Niño occurs when the ocean water off the west coast of South America gets warmer. This causes heavy rain and flooding in South America and drought in Asia and Australia. La Niña has the opposite effect. When the water off the west coast of South America cools, it brings torrential rain to Australia and Asia, and drought to South America.

GLOSSARY

atmosphere The thin layer of gases that surrounds planets such as the Earth.

cold front The leading edge of a moving mass of cold air.

equator An imaginary line around the world that lies halfway between the North and South Poles.

meteorologist A person who studies the weather conditions and uses them to forecast the weather.

occluded front A combination of a cold front and a warm front.

sleet A mixture of snow and rain.

solar energy The energy that comes from the Sun.

thermometer An instrument that measures air temperature.

warm front The leading edge of a moving mass of warm air.

weather forecast A prediction of what the weather might be in the near future.

INDEX

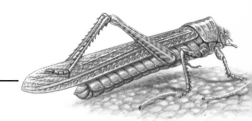

PICTURE AND ILLUSTRATION CREDITS

[t=top, b=bottom, l=left, r=right, c=center, F=front, B=back, C=cover, bg=background]

Mike Atkinson/illustration 10l, 12tl, 12cl, 12bc, 12–13bc, 31tr. **Andrew Beckett/illustration** 3br, 24–25c, 29tr. **Jean-Loup Charmet** 6bl. **Corel Corporation** 11cl, 11tr, 13tl, 16rc, 20tr, 20cr, 20lc, 21lc, 23tr, 25tl, 25cr, 29cl, 4–32 borders, Cbg. **Davis Instruments** 16tl. **Digital Stock** 5bl, 29br. **Mike Gorman** 8–9rc. **Ray Grinaway** 23bc. **Lorraine Hannay** 14l, 17r, FCc. **Richard Hook/Bernard Thornton Artists UK** 6–7rc. **Trevor Keeling** 19br. **David Kirshner** 25br. **Jillian Luff** 22tl, 22tc, 24cl, 27tr, 27tl. **Rob Mancini** 1c, 26bc. **Iain McKellar** 5c. **PhotoEssentials** 20–21bc, 20tl, 21bc, 21br. **Tony Pyrzakowski** 4–5tc. **Oliver Rennert** 2tl, 18–19lc. **Trevor Ruth** 22–23c, 26tc. **Michael Saunders** 27bc. **Stephen Seymour/Bernard Thornton Artists UK** 28bc. **Oliver Strewe** 15tl, 15bl, 15c, 16bl, 30bl. **The Photo Library—Sydney/NASA/Science Photo Library** 8bl. **Steve Trevaskis** 19cr.

BOOKS IN THIS SERIES

WEIRD AND WONDERFUL WILDLIFE

Incredible Creatures
Creepy Creatures
Scaly Things
Feathers and Flight
Attack and Defense
Snakes
Hidden World
Reptiles and Amphibians
Mini Mammals
Up and Away
Mighty Mammals
Dangerous Animals

LAND, SEA, AND SKY

Sharks and Rays
Underwater Animals
Mammals of the Sea
Ocean Life
Volcanoes
Weather Watching
Maps and Our World
Earthquakes
The Plant Kingdom
Rain or Shine
Sky Watch
The Planets

INFORMATION STATION

Every Body Tells a Story
The Human Body
Bright Ideas
Out and About
Exploring Space
High Flying
How Things Work
Native Americans
Travelers and Traders
Sports for All
People from the Past
Play Ball!